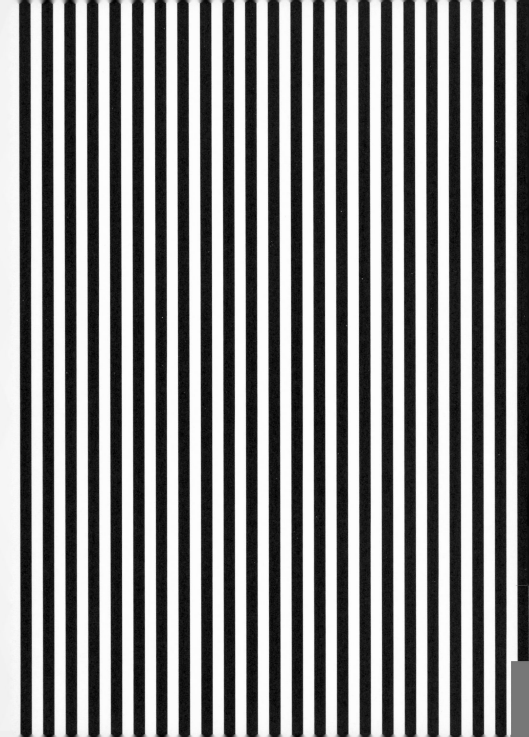

"Gratitude is the sign of noble souls."

Aesop (620–564 BC), ancient Greek storyteller

This journal is dedicated to the people, places, and patterns that inspire us all to live more positive and purposeful lives. We are infinitely grateful.

# BE GREAT
# BE GRATEFUL

A Gratitude Journal for Positive Living

**Andrews McMeel**
PUBLISHING®

# Gratitude

ˈgratɪtjuːd/

noun

"The quality of being thankful; readiness to show appreciation for and to return kindness."
*Oxford English Dictionary*

Gratitude comes from the Latin word *gratia*, meaning grace, graciousness, or gratefulness.

# Finding More Excellence Every Day

## Excellence really is everywhere — we just need to go outside and see it.

Being aware, grateful, and appreciative … sounds simple, but it's easy to take things for granted. How can we begin to create more gratitude not just for the obviously excellent but also for the mundane everyday that we all too often overlook?

Gratitude is powerful. It makes us feel happier, healthier, and more hopeful. Life flows when we are more grateful. And it's not just us who benefit. Imbuing our lives with daily gratitude has the power to ripple outward to everyone and everything we come into contact with.

So join us on an empowering voyage of exploration from drain-cover-spotting to cosmic pondering, simple observations to nature immersions, as we look at inspiring and innovative ways to invite more gratitude into our daily lives.

We hope you enjoy the journal as much as we enjoyed putting it together.

Anna + Grace, PATTERNITY cofounders

# Contents

## An Introduction

## A Continuation

## Phase 1. Mundane

## Phase 2. Me

## Phase 3. Magnificent

## Daily Gratitude Logs

Designed to help you to harness
the power of gratitude each day,
both morning and night.
26–173

## Pattern Ponderings

See and appreciate everyday
details with fresh eyes.
31, 81, 131

## Mantras and
## Inspirational Quotes

Words to inspire and empower,
brought to you by some of the
greatest minds in history.
1–192

## Pause + Reflect

Break the autopilot and create
new patterns of appreciation.
42, 47, 68, 103, 118,
147, 164, 169

## Grateful Explorations

Venture deeper into your
grateful journey.
36, 56, 86, 114, 136, 158

## Free-Flow Pages

Blank pages for you to share
your observations, write, draw,
create, and explore …
186–191

# Why Gratitude —
# Why Now?

# "Wealth is the ability to fully experience life."

Henry David Thoreau (1817–1862), poet

Today's culture can often feel out of balance. We are bombarded by information and overloaded with stuff. We compare ourselves to others daily — often before we've even gotten out of bed. And the data is now in. Scientific research has confirmed that after a certain point (once our basic needs for food, clothing, shelter, medical care, education, and transportation are covered) the increasing affluence in the West over the last few generations has had no correlation with our happiness or well-being. So what does this actually mean? Is our belief in the power of the material waning? Is confusing our human needs with our perpetual wants doing us more harm than good? Perhaps it's time to reassess our patterns of thinking and doing — and start creating some new ones.

Since launching in 2009, our creative organization PATTERNITY has been researching the inspirational power of pattern through projects and experiments that explore the relationship between pattern and well-being. We started out as an open-access social platform that sought to inspire people to slow down and simply notice more — encouraging a heightened appreciation of the visual beauty of the everyday, from the drain covers beneath our feet to the cloud formations above our heads. Over the years we have learned that this mindful way of living can create a way of seeing that drives moments of curiosity and calm amidst the complexity. We have also conceived events, and designed projects and products that encourage people to venture beneath the surface and consider the interconnected patterns and systems that shape life. It has been heartening to observe how this has led to an appreciation of not only the design of our immediate surroundings, but also the design of our own bodies, minds, and natural environments — of which we are a delicate, interwoven part.

We believe pattern can be an empowering and inspiring lens with which to help people design more positive and purposeful lives. And that's exactly what this journal is all about.

# Flow

## noun

## /fləʊ/

1. The condition of proceeding or being produced continuously and effortlessly
2. The act of going from one place to another in a steady stream

Being in flow is to feel fully absorbed in present-moment awareness. To experience flow is to dissolve boundaries and sense the interrelatedness of all things; to feel connected to a greater whole — e.g., *She felt like life was in flow when she lived each day with more gratitude.*

## The Power of Flow

As a company that specializes in design, we are often thinking about how and why things work. Whether that's our external environment, the inner workings of our own bodies, or the wider system and relationships of which we are all a part. It's often only when a system breaks down or something is taken away from us that we realize how grateful we were for it, how much it made our lives effortlessly flow, and perhaps how much we took it for granted. This is at the root of our first journal exploring the power of gratitude for not just the excellent but also the everyday — to drive positivity and flow through developing everyday awareness, inner understanding, and a wider perspective.

# Gratitude — the Benefits

Fostering an attitude of gratitude has been proven time and again to increase happiness and well-being. Here are just a few of the scientifically recognized benefits of finding more excellence every day. We invite you to circle the benefits you would like to focus on during your grateful journey:

## GRATITUDE = IMPROVED

| | |
|---|---|
| Health | Inspiration |
| Sense of purpose | Learning |
| Relationships | Wonder |
| Compassion | Play |
| Resilience | Love |
| Sleep | Joy |
| Creativity | Serenity |
| Confidence | Hope |
| Clarity | Meaning |
| Balance | Kindness |

∞ We've left some space here for you to set some positive intentions for your goals. (e.g., It would be great if I could invite more ... into my life because I would feel ...)

# 10 Steps to Grateful Living

"Give thanks for unknown blessings
already on their way."

Native American saying

Many of the world's greatest scientific and spiritual masters from Einstein to Gandhi considered gratitude to be one of the greatest virtues; one that can help everyone on their journey toward greatness. Here's a list of 10 suggestions for how to invite the power of gratitude into your life each day:

1. Take a moment to fully welcome the wonder of each new day
2. Tune in to the sustainability of your everyday habits and processes
3. Appreciate moments of awareness and clarity
4. Reconsider the things you use and often take for granted
5. Create space to tune in and care for your body and inner system

6. Be curious and open to learn anew and venture into the unknown
7. Find ways to accept challenges as opportunities for personal growth
8. Take time to nurture your relationship with the natural world
9. Remember you are part of and supported by a complex web of life
10. Create ways to say thank you, strengthen your connections, and give back

# How This Journal Works

"Happiness is a good flow of life."

Zeno of Citium (c.334–262 BC), Greek philosopher

Through three core phases — featuring gratitude logs, creative exercises, playful prompts, uplifting quotes, free-flow pages, and thoughtful suggestions — this journal will help you to become more aware of, and better understand, your thought patterns, inspiring simple ways to create new behaviors that shape your contentment and appreciation every day.

First we ask you to become more aware, more appreciative, and find beauty and inspiration in the everyday. Secondly, to think about design not just in terms of patterned visuals or products, but how to be tuned in to the inner patterns deep within us, from our individual patterns of thinking and doing. Finally we ask you to think about how you connect and interact with something greater — the wider patterns that make up our societies and culture. How might this feeling of interconnectivity change the way you interact with your environment, other people, and indeed yourself? What new patterns of thinking or behavior might this inspire?

Completing this journal will provide you with the tools you need to feel more connected to yourself and the wider world. Implementing our ongoing pattern research — from modern science to the wisdom of ancient spirituality — it has been conceived and designed with one core mission: to empower you to develop more meaningful and productive ways of working and living, find purpose, and improve your happiness and well-being.

# Check In

## Recognizing Your Personal Pattern

Thank you for reading our journal introduction. You're just about ready to get started. But before you begin, please start by just taking a few moments to check in and reflect on where you are right now in your life. (We'll be repeating this exercise again once you've finished the journal to notice what positive changes have taken place.)

How balanced are the different areas that make up the whole? In other words, is the work section full but free time empty? Are you happy with your levels of family and friendship? What are your priorities right now, and does that match the shape you are currently seeing? If not, what areas might you want to nourish more? Keep this in mind as you go through the journal and see if things change when we reach the end.

My life pattern: outline your
current level of contentment
with the below.

Health
Purpose
Free Time
Work
Finances
Friendship
Family
Home

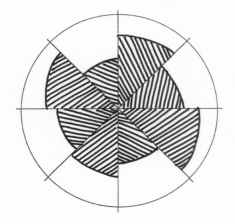

∞ Try not to judge your pattern or be critical if things don't feel as you'd like them to be — just become aware of the shape and appreciate the perspective it will give you as you set out on your grateful journey.

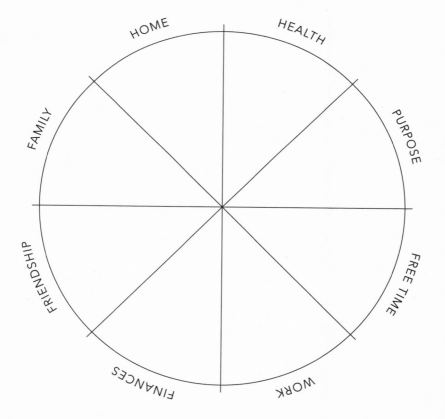

# The Grateful Journey

### STEP 1
### AWARENESS

Join us as we become more alive to the
excellence of the everyday — driving a
more playful and positive way of seeing and
engaging with our daily surroundings.

### STEP 2
### UNDERSTANDING

Dig beneath the surface as we seek to better
understand our own bodies and minds —
inspiring a deeper awareness and appreciation
of our physical and unseen patterns.

### STEP 3
### CONNECTION

Expand your perspective as we begin to
cultivate a renewed sense of wonder for the
wider relationships and connections that
support and give meaning to our lives.

# Introducing Your Daily Grateful Pages

Your grateful journey starts on page 26 when you reach your first daily grateful log. These pages are an essential part of your grateful tool kit, encouraging you to get into the habit of gratitude at the start and end of each day. Use these pages to log your daily observations, appreciations, and importantly, to set new intentions to positively shape your life pattern.

A blank page can be intimidating, so here's some inspiration and guidance to get you started:

Date:

**(A)**

MORNING CHECK-IN ○

I'm feeling:

**(B)**

Reasons to be grateful today

1.
2.
3.

**(C)**

What would make today great?

1.
2.
3.

**(D)**

EVENING REFLECTION ●

I'm feeling:

**(E)**

Great things that happened today

1.
2.
3.

## Ⓐ Morning Check-In

Start each new day by checking in and recognizing the feelings that arise each morning. Resist judging these as either "good" or "bad," but simply be curious as to what emerges for you.

## Ⓑ Reasons to Be Grateful Today

Fill these spaces with moments of gratitude from the mundane to the magnificent. These might include:

1. The wonder of your everyday surroundings:
- A dappled shadow through your window at work
- A really great cup of tea
- Going to bed in clean sheets

2. The wisdom of your inner world:
- Laughing out loud with a friend
- Waking up feeling energized and positive
- Learning something new after a negative experience

3. Your wider relationships, community, and connections:
- A glowing full moon on a clear night
- Being able to see the stars, hear birdsong, smell the sea
- Helping someone in need

## Ⓒ What Would Make Today Great?

Look further and visualize a positive pattern for the day ahead; set an intention and clarify how today can be great.

## Ⓓ Evening Reflection

Take a few moments in the evening to reflect. Try listing the emotions you would like to feel in addition to the ones you are already experiencing; writing positive words and affirmations is a proven way to invite powerful new patterns of behavior into your life.

## Ⓔ Great Things That Happened Today

A final chance to recognize the 3 greatest things that happened to you that day. Take a pause of appreciation before starting a new day.

∞ Your pages needn't take more than 5 minutes per day. Once in the morning and again before bed. It will be the best 300 seconds you ever spent!

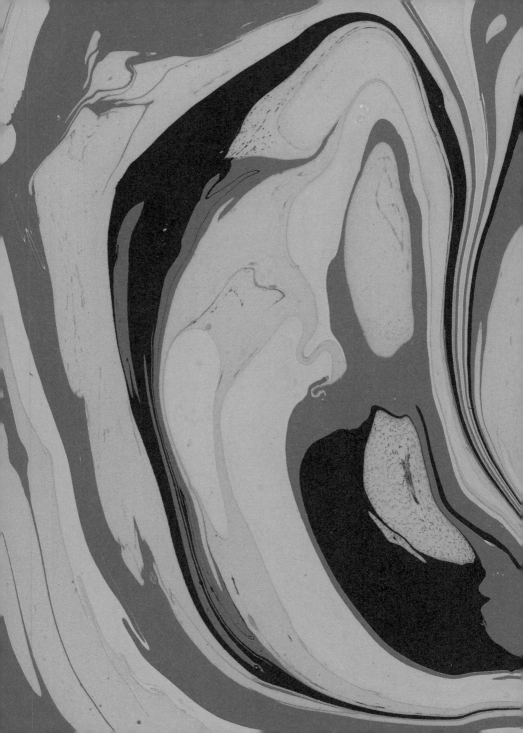

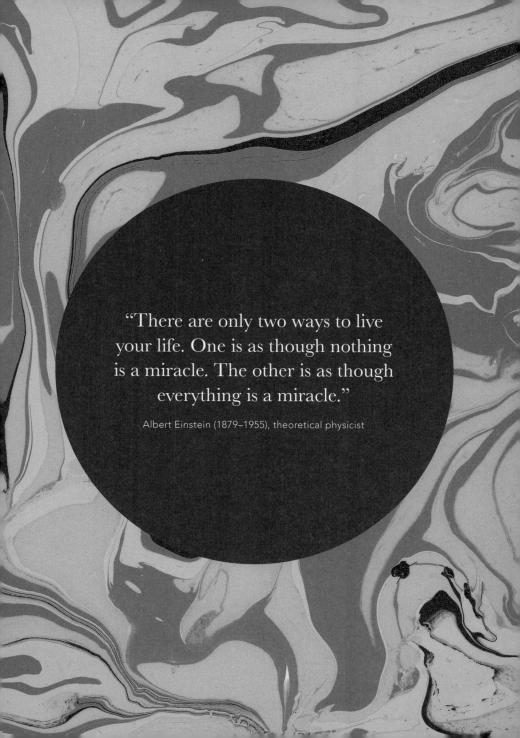

"There are only two ways to live your life. One is as though nothing is a miracle. The other is as though everything is a miracle."

Albert Einstein (1879–1955), theoretical physicist

# Mundane

## Generating Everyday Awareness + Appreciation

We can last roughly three minutes without air, three hours without warmth, three days without water, and three weeks without food. How many other things can we not live without — but often fail to appreciate in the daily rush from a to b? This first chapter seeks to set you on the grateful journey by observing the often overlooked with a renewed curiosity and awareness. The aim? To encourage a more playful and positive way of seeing and experiencing the everyday world around you. Let's start with the patterns of our immediate surroundings.

Date:

## MORNING CHECK-IN ○

I'm feeling:

......................................................................................................

......................................................................................................

### Reasons to be grateful today

1. .................................................................................................

2. .................................................................................................

3. .................................................................................................

### What would make today great?

1. .................................................................................................

2. .................................................................................................

3. .................................................................................................

## EVENING REFLECTION ●

I'm feeling:

......................................................................................................

......................................................................................................

### Great things that happened today

1. .................................................................................................

2. .................................................................................................

3. .................................................................................................

Date:

## MORNING CHECK-IN ○

I'm feeling:

........................................................................................................

........................................................................................................

### Reasons to be grateful today

1. ..................................................................................................

2. ..................................................................................................

3. ..................................................................................................

### What would make today great?

1. ..................................................................................................

2. ..................................................................................................

3. ..................................................................................................

## EVENING REFLECTION ●

I'm feeling:

........................................................................................................

........................................................................................................

### Great things that happened today

1. ..................................................................................................

2. ..................................................................................................

3. ..................................................................................................

Date:

## MORNING CHECK-IN ○

I'm feeling:
..............................................................................................

..............................................................................................

### Reasons to be grateful today

1. ..........................................................................................
2. ..........................................................................................
3. ..........................................................................................

### What would make today great?

1. ..........................................................................................
2. ..........................................................................................
3. ..........................................................................................

## EVENING REFLECTION ●

I'm feeling:
..............................................................................................

..............................................................................................

### Great things that happened today

1. ..........................................................................................
2. ..........................................................................................
3. ..........................................................................................

Date:

## MORNING CHECK-IN ○

I'm feeling:
........................................................................................................
........................................................................................................

### Reasons to be grateful today

1. ........................................................................................................
2. ........................................................................................................
3. ........................................................................................................

### What would make today great?

1. ........................................................................................................
2. ........................................................................................................
3. ........................................................................................................

## EVENING REFLECTION ●

I'm feeling:
........................................................................................................
........................................................................................................

### Great things that happened today

1. ........................................................................................................
2. ........................................................................................................
3. ........................................................................................................

# Pattern Pondering No. 1

## Opening Our Eyes

From dappled bananas and turquoise stripy shutters to a cosmic constellation of bubbles that emerged in your glass overnight, inspirational everyday encounters really are everywhere. We just need to open our eyes to see them. Look closer, see more, and share your own moments with us @patternity.

"The present moment is filled with joy and happiness. If you are attentive, you will see it."

Thích Nhât Hanh (b.1926), Zen Buddhist monk

Date:

## MORNING CHECK-IN ○

I'm feeling:
...................................................................................................................

...................................................................................................................

### Reasons to be grateful today

1. ...............................................................................................................

2. ...............................................................................................................

3. ...............................................................................................................

### What would make today great?

1. ...............................................................................................................

2. ...............................................................................................................

3. ...............................................................................................................

## EVENING REFLECTION ●

I'm feeling:
...................................................................................................................

...................................................................................................................

### Great things that happened today

1. ...............................................................................................................

2. ...............................................................................................................

3. ...............................................................................................................

Date:

## MORNING CHECK-IN ○

I'm feeling:

........................................................................................................................

........................................................................................................................

### Reasons to be grateful today

1. ........................................................................................................................

2. ........................................................................................................................

3. ........................................................................................................................

### What would make today great?

1. ........................................................................................................................

2. ........................................................................................................................

3. ........................................................................................................................

## EVENING REFLECTION ●

I'm feeling:

........................................................................................................................

........................................................................................................................

### Great things that happened today

1. ........................................................................................................................

2. ........................................................................................................................

3. ........................................................................................................................

Date:

## MORNING CHECK-IN ○

I'm feeling:

........................................................................................................

........................................................................................................

### Reasons to be grateful today

1. ....................................................................................................

2. ....................................................................................................

3. ....................................................................................................

### What would make today great?

1. ....................................................................................................

2. ....................................................................................................

3. ....................................................................................................

## EVENING REFLECTION ●

I'm feeling:

........................................................................................................

........................................................................................................

### Great things that happened today

1. ....................................................................................................

2. ....................................................................................................

3. ....................................................................................................

Date:

## MORNING CHECK-IN ○

I'm feeling:

........................................................................................................................

........................................................................................................................

### Reasons to be grateful today

1.
........................................................................................................................
2.
........................................................................................................................
3.
........................................................................................................................

### What would make today great?

1.
........................................................................................................................
2.
........................................................................................................................
3.
........................................................................................................................

## EVENING REFLECTION ●

I'm feeling:

........................................................................................................................

........................................................................................................................

### Great things that happened today

1.
........................................................................................................................
2.
........................................................................................................................
3.
........................................................................................................................

# Grateful Exploration No. 1

Break the Autopilot — Morning Greeting | 5 minutes

## "Let us be thankful for that which is."

William Shakespeare (1564–1616), playwright

Four out of five smartphone users check their phones within the first 15 minutes of waking up. 80 percent of those say it's the first thing they do in the morning. Instead of racing straight into your morning routine today, try taking just a few moments to fully welcome the wonder of a new day here on planet Earth (after all, it's taken over 4.5 billion years for us to get here).

## PREPARATION

Find a quiet, comfortable seat where you will not be disturbed.
Put your feet flat on the floor, knees bent, hips at a right angle to your ankles.
Sit with your spine straight but relaxed, your hands resting in your lap palms up.
Eyes gently open.
First tune in to the support beneath you.
Notice the quality of the light in the room.
Take several deep, full breaths, breathing through your nose, into

your lungs, into your stomach, and then out through your mouth.
Notice the smell of your surroundings. Tune in to the pattern of the sounds around you.
Take a final, full, deep inhalation and exhalation.
Stretch your arms above your head. Raise your chin to the sky.
Say thank you for the opportunity of this new day.

Consider making this the start of your daily pattern and see how you feel after a few days, weeks, months …

## OBSERVATION

How did this make you feel? What came up? What did you notice in your body?

Why not explore your experience on the free-flow pages at the back of the journal?

Search "grateful" via Patternity.org to listen to this as guided meditation

Date:

## MORNING CHECK-IN ○

I'm feeling:
.................................................................................................
.................................................................................................

### Reasons to be grateful today

1. ..............................................................................................
2. ..............................................................................................
3. ..............................................................................................

### What would make today great?

1. ..............................................................................................
2. ..............................................................................................
3. ..............................................................................................

## EVENING REFLECTION ●

I'm feeling:
.................................................................................................
.................................................................................................

### Great things that happened today

1. ..............................................................................................
2. ..............................................................................................
3. ..............................................................................................

Date:

## MORNING CHECK-IN ○

I'm feeling:

........................................................................................

........................................................................................

### Reasons to be grateful today

1. ........................................................................................

2. ........................................................................................

3. ........................................................................................

### What would make today great?

1. ........................................................................................

2. ........................................................................................

3. ........................................................................................

## EVENING REFLECTION ●

I'm feeling:

........................................................................................

........................................................................................

### Great things that happened today

1. ........................................................................................

2. ........................................................................................

3. ........................................................................................

Date:

## MORNING CHECK-IN ○

I'm feeling:
.......................................................................................................
.......................................................................................................

### Reasons to be grateful today

1. ...............................................................................................
2. ...............................................................................................
3. ...............................................................................................

### What would make today great?

1. ...............................................................................................
2. ...............................................................................................
3. ...............................................................................................

## EVENING REFLECTION ●

I'm feeling:
.......................................................................................................
.......................................................................................................

### Great things that happened today

1. ...............................................................................................
2. ...............................................................................................
3. ...............................................................................................

Date:

## MORNING CHECK-IN ○

I'm feeling:
........................................................................................................................

........................................................................................................................

### Reasons to be grateful today

1. ........................................................................................................................

2. ........................................................................................................................

3. ........................................................................................................................

### What would make today great?

1. ........................................................................................................................

2. ........................................................................................................................

3. ........................................................................................................................

## EVENING REFLECTION ●

I'm feeling:
........................................................................................................................

........................................................................................................................

### Great things that happened today

1. ........................................................................................................................

2. ........................................................................................................................

3. ........................................................................................................................

( II )

# Pause + Reflect

## Daily Design

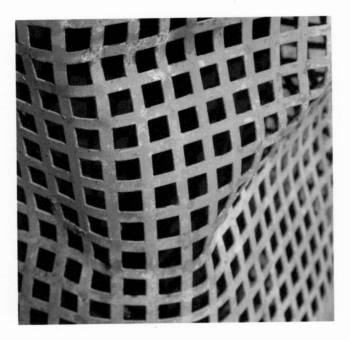

How much everyday design goes completely unnoticed? Today try observing a chair, a pen, a teacup, a trash can or any design piece that you use daily, as if it was the first time. Think about all the ways it helps you. Take a moment to thank it for its service to you.

Date:

## MORNING CHECK-IN ○

I'm feeling:
......................................................................................................................

......................................................................................................................

### Reasons to be grateful today

1. ......................................................................................................................
2. ......................................................................................................................
3. ......................................................................................................................

### What would make today great?

1. ......................................................................................................................
2. ......................................................................................................................
3. ......................................................................................................................

## EVENING REFLECTION ●

I'm feeling:
......................................................................................................................

......................................................................................................................

### Great things that happened today

1. ......................................................................................................................
2. ......................................................................................................................
3. ......................................................................................................................

Date:

## MORNING CHECK-IN    ○

I'm feeling:
.................................................................................................

.................................................................................................

### Reasons to be grateful today

1. ...............................................................................................
2. ...............................................................................................
3. ...............................................................................................

### What would make today great?

1. ...............................................................................................
2. ...............................................................................................
3. ...............................................................................................

## EVENING REFLECTION    ●

I'm feeling:
.................................................................................................

.................................................................................................

### Great things that happened today

1. ...............................................................................................
2. ...............................................................................................
3. ...............................................................................................

Date:

## MORNING CHECK-IN  ○

I'm feeling:
............................................................................
............................................................................

### Reasons to be grateful today

1. ...........................................................................
2. ...........................................................................
3. ...........................................................................

### What would make today great?

1. ...........................................................................
2. ...........................................................................
3. ...........................................................................

## EVENING REFLECTION  ●

I'm feeling:
............................................................................
............................................................................

### Great things that happened today

1. ...........................................................................
2. ...........................................................................
3. ...........................................................................

Date:

## MORNING CHECK-IN ○

I'm feeling:
......................................................................................................................................................
......................................................................................................................................................

### Reasons to be grateful today

1. ...............................................................................................................................................
2. ...............................................................................................................................................
3. ...............................................................................................................................................

### What would make today great?

1. ...............................................................................................................................................
2. ...............................................................................................................................................
3. ...............................................................................................................................................

## EVENING REFLECTION ●

I'm feeling:
......................................................................................................................................................
......................................................................................................................................................

### Great things that happened today

1. ...............................................................................................................................................
2. ...............................................................................................................................................
3. ...............................................................................................................................................

# Pause + Reflect

## Water

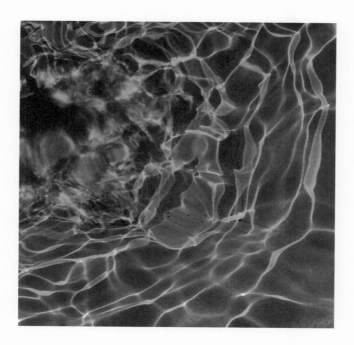

In the United States every person uses approximately 80 to 100 gallons of water a day. Today take note of how much water you use to drink, cook with, wash the dishes, flush the toilet, water the plants … Take a moment to appreciate the flow of water in and out of your life.

Date:

## MORNING CHECK-IN ◯

I'm feeling:

.............................................................................

.............................................................................

### Reasons to be grateful today

1. ..........................................................................
2. ..........................................................................
3. ..........................................................................

### What would make today great?

1. ..........................................................................
2. ..........................................................................
3. ..........................................................................

## EVENING REFLECTION ●

I'm feeling:

.............................................................................

.............................................................................

### Great things that happened today

1. ..........................................................................
2. ..........................................................................
3. ..........................................................................

Date:

## MORNING CHECK-IN ○

I'm feeling:

........................................................................................................

........................................................................................................

### Reasons to be grateful today

1. ........................................................................................

2. ........................................................................................

3. ........................................................................................

### What would make today great?

1. ........................................................................................

2. ........................................................................................

3. ........................................................................................

## EVENING REFLECTION ●

I'm feeling:

........................................................................................................

........................................................................................................

### Great things that happened today

1. ........................................................................................

2. ........................................................................................

3. ........................................................................................

# DELIGHT
# IN
# DAILY
# DETAILS

Date:

## MORNING CHECK-IN ○

I'm feeling:

......................................................................................................................................

......................................................................................................................................

### Reasons to be grateful today

1.
......................................................................................................................................

2.
......................................................................................................................................

3.
......................................................................................................................................

### What would make today great?

1.
......................................................................................................................................

2.
......................................................................................................................................

3.
......................................................................................................................................

## EVENING REFLECTION ●

I'm feeling:

......................................................................................................................................

......................................................................................................................................

### Great things that happened today

1.
......................................................................................................................................

2.
......................................................................................................................................

3.
......................................................................................................................................

Date:

## MORNING CHECK-IN ○

I'm feeling:

.........................................................................................................

.........................................................................................................

### Reasons to be grateful today

1.
...........................................................................................................

2.
...........................................................................................................

3.
...........................................................................................................

### What would make today great?

1.
...........................................................................................................

2.
...........................................................................................................

3.
...........................................................................................................

## EVENING REFLECTION ●

I'm feeling:

.........................................................................................................

.........................................................................................................

### Great things that happened today

1.
...........................................................................................................

2.
...........................................................................................................

3.
...........................................................................................................

Date:

## MORNING CHECK-IN ○

I'm feeling:

.........................................................................................................

.........................................................................................................

### Reasons to be grateful today

1. ...................................................................................................

2. ...................................................................................................

3. ...................................................................................................

### What would make today great?

1. ...................................................................................................

2. ...................................................................................................

3. ...................................................................................................

## EVENING REFLECTION ●

I'm feeling:

.........................................................................................................

.........................................................................................................

### Great things that happened today

1. ...................................................................................................

2. ...................................................................................................

3. ...................................................................................................

Date:

## MORNING CHECK-IN ○

I'm feeling:
..................................................................................................................

..................................................................................................................

### Reasons to be grateful today

1. ...............................................................................................................
2. ...............................................................................................................
3. ...............................................................................................................

### What would make today great?

1. ...............................................................................................................
2. ...............................................................................................................
3. ...............................................................................................................

## EVENING REFLECTION ●

I'm feeling:
..................................................................................................................

..................................................................................................................

### Great things that happened today

1. ...............................................................................................................
2. ...............................................................................................................
3. ...............................................................................................................

# Grateful Exploration No. 2

Brighten Up Your Commute — Follow a Pattern | 1 hour

## "It's not what you look at that matters, it's what you see."

Henry David Thoreau (1817–1862), American poet

The average city commuter encounters over 2,000 ads per day. Often we're so rushed to get to our destination that we fail to widen our perspective and appreciate the journey. Have you ever stopped to notice the shapes, objects, and patterns that add together to make up our daily environment? Maybe they are functional — lines to keep us safe, squares to stack, spots to signal the way; or perhaps they are decorative, adding beautiful touches to things we often overlook. Some will be both.

## PREPARATION

Today try looking out for the simple shapes and patterns that surround you, and notice how they occur in everything that is around us — from square window grids and circular drain covers to stripy shadows. Notice all the forms of the world around you, and how they connect to create functions and flow.

If you have time, try letting a shape, like a circle, lead the way. Let your curiosity and intuition lead you as you observe up close and far away. Let yourself meander and see where it leads.

## OBSERVATION

How does it feel to let something else dictate where you look or what path you take? What did you see? Did you discover something new? Where did it take you?

Liked spotting circles? Next why not try stripes, grids, waves …

Try writing or drawing your experience in your free-flow pages at the back of the journal.

Share your pattern discoveries with us via Instagram: @patternity #BeGreatBeGrateful

Date:

## MORNING CHECK-IN ○

I'm feeling:

.................................................................................................

.................................................................................................

### Reasons to be grateful today

1. ..............................................................................................
2. ..............................................................................................
3. ..............................................................................................

### What would make today great?

1. ..............................................................................................
2. ..............................................................................................
3. ..............................................................................................

## EVENING REFLECTION ●

I'm feeling:

.................................................................................................

.................................................................................................

### Great things that happened today

1. ..............................................................................................
2. ..............................................................................................
3. ..............................................................................................

Date:

## MORNING CHECK-IN ○

I'm feeling:

........................................................................................................

........................................................................................................

### Reasons to be grateful today

1. ..................................................................................................

2. ..................................................................................................

3. ..................................................................................................

### What would make today great?

1. ..................................................................................................

2. ..................................................................................................

3. ..................................................................................................

## EVENING REFLECTION ●

I'm feeling:

........................................................................................................

........................................................................................................

### Great things that happened today

1. ..................................................................................................

2. ..................................................................................................

3. ..................................................................................................

Date:

## MORNING CHECK-IN ○

I'm feeling:
.............................................................................

.............................................................................

### Reasons to be grateful today

1. .........................................................................
2. .........................................................................
3. .........................................................................

### What would make today great?

1. .........................................................................
2. .........................................................................
3. .........................................................................

## EVENING REFLECTION ●

I'm feeling:
.............................................................................

.............................................................................

### Great things that happened today

1. .........................................................................
2. .........................................................................
3. .........................................................................

Date:

## MORNING CHECK-IN     ○

I'm feeling:
........................................................................................
........................................................................................

### Reasons to be grateful today

1. ........................................................................................
2. ........................................................................................
3. ........................................................................................

### What would make today great?

1. ........................................................................................
2. ........................................................................................
3. ........................................................................................

## EVENING REFLECTION     ●

I'm feeling:
........................................................................................
........................................................................................

### Great things that happened today

1. ........................................................................................
2. ........................................................................................
3. ........................................................................................

# ENJOY
# EVERYDAY
# EXCELLENCE

Date:

## MORNING CHECK-IN ○

I'm feeling:
...................................................................................................
...................................................................................................

### Reasons to be grateful today

1. ...............................................................................................
2. ...............................................................................................
3. ...............................................................................................

### What would make today great?

1. ...............................................................................................
2. ...............................................................................................
3. ...............................................................................................

## EVENING REFLECTION ●

I'm feeling:
...................................................................................................
...................................................................................................

### Great things that happened today

1. ...............................................................................................
2. ...............................................................................................
3. ...............................................................................................

Date:

## MORNING CHECK-IN ○

I'm feeling:
..............................................................................................................................

..............................................................................................................................

### Reasons to be grateful today

1.
..............................................................................................................................
2.
..............................................................................................................................
3.
..............................................................................................................................

### What would make today great?

1.
..............................................................................................................................
2.
..............................................................................................................................
3.
..............................................................................................................................

## EVENING REFLECTION ●

I'm feeling:
..............................................................................................................................

..............................................................................................................................

### Great things that happened today

1.
..............................................................................................................................
2.
..............................................................................................................................
3.
..............................................................................................................................

Date:

## MORNING CHECK-IN ○

I'm feeling:
.......................................................................................................................................
.......................................................................................................................................

### Reasons to be grateful today

1. ................................................................................................................................
2. ................................................................................................................................
3. ................................................................................................................................

### What would make today great?

1. ................................................................................................................................
2. ................................................................................................................................
3. ................................................................................................................................

## EVENING REFLECTION ●

I'm feeling:
.......................................................................................................................................
.......................................................................................................................................

### Great things that happened today

1. ................................................................................................................................
2. ................................................................................................................................
3. ................................................................................................................................

Date:

## MORNING CHECK-IN ○

I'm feeling:

.............................................................................................................

.............................................................................................................

### Reasons to be grateful today

1. .........................................................................................................

2. .........................................................................................................

3. .........................................................................................................

### What would make today great?

1. .........................................................................................................

2. .........................................................................................................

3. .........................................................................................................

## EVENING REFLECTION ●

I'm feeling:

.............................................................................................................

.............................................................................................................

### Great things that happened today

1. .........................................................................................................

2. .........................................................................................................

3. .........................................................................................................

## (II)

# Pause + Reflect

## Simplicity

Cultures across the globe from Indian monks to American neuroscientists speak of the benefits of switching off in order to fully engage with the present moment. In an overstretched, ever-connected world it can feel difficult to do just one thing at a time. Today try breaking the pattern of multitasking and enjoy the experience of focusing on one thing at a time: eating your dinner without digital distractions, reading a book minus endless notifications, walking in the park and listening to the birds …

Date:

## MORNING CHECK-IN ○

I'm feeling:

........................................................................................

........................................................................................

### Reasons to be grateful today

1. ........................................................................................

2. ........................................................................................

3. ........................................................................................

### What would make today great?

1. ........................................................................................

2. ........................................................................................

3. ........................................................................................

## EVENING REFLECTION ●

I'm feeling:

........................................................................................

........................................................................................

### Great things that happened today

1. ........................................................................................

2. ........................................................................................

3. ........................................................................................

Date:

## MORNING CHECK-IN  ○

I'm feeling:

......................................................................................................

......................................................................................................

### Reasons to be grateful today

1. ................................................................................................

2. ................................................................................................

3. ................................................................................................

### What would make today great?

1. ................................................................................................

2. ................................................................................................

3. ................................................................................................

## EVENING REFLECTION  ●

I'm feeling:

......................................................................................................

......................................................................................................

### Great things that happened today

1. ................................................................................................

2. ................................................................................................

3. ................................................................................................

Date:

## MORNING CHECK-IN ○

I'm feeling:
......................................................................................................................................................................

......................................................................................................................................................................

### Reasons to be grateful today

1. ....................................................................................................................................................................

2. ....................................................................................................................................................................

3. ....................................................................................................................................................................

### What would make today great?

1. ....................................................................................................................................................................

2. ....................................................................................................................................................................

3. ....................................................................................................................................................................

## EVENING REFLECTION ●

I'm feeling:
......................................................................................................................................................................

......................................................................................................................................................................

### Great things that happened today

1. ....................................................................................................................................................................

2. ....................................................................................................................................................................

3. ....................................................................................................................................................................

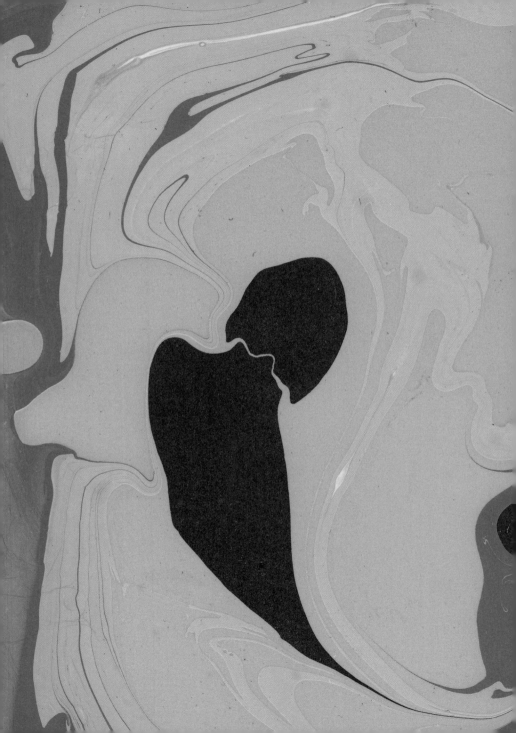

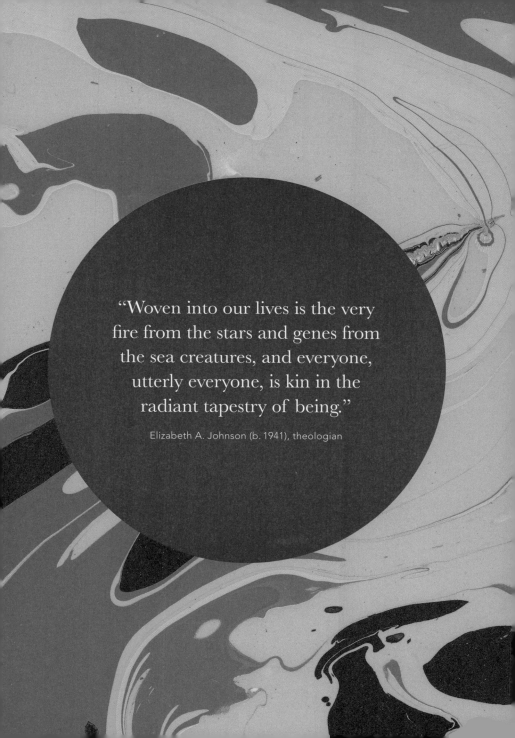

"Woven into our lives is the very fire from the stars and genes from the sea creatures, and everyone, utterly everyone, is kin in the radiant tapestry of being."

Elizabeth A. Johnson (b. 1941), theologian

# PHASE 2.

# Me

## Understanding Our Inner World + the Unseen

Now that we've looked at the external world around us, it's time to venture beneath the surface and foster a new appreciation for the very personal world we inhabit — our own bodies and minds. From a heart that beats for a lifetime, a mind that is active 24 hours a day, an immune system of millions of cells working harmoniously together, and a constellation of emotions and hormones that shape our growth and resilience, this chapter seeks to inspire an empowering curiosity and awareness as we tap into the power of the microcosm within.

Date:

## MORNING CHECK-IN ◯

I'm feeling:

........................................................................................

........................................................................................

### Reasons to be grateful today

1. ....................................................................................
2. ....................................................................................
3. ....................................................................................

### What would make today great?

1. ....................................................................................
2. ....................................................................................
3. ....................................................................................

## EVENING REFLECTION ●

I'm feeling:

........................................................................................

........................................................................................

### Great things that happened today

1. ....................................................................................
2. ....................................................................................
3. ....................................................................................

Date:

## MORNING CHECK-IN ○

I'm feeling:
...............................................................................................................................
...............................................................................................................................

### Reasons to be grateful today

1. ...............................................................................................................................
2. ...............................................................................................................................
3. ...............................................................................................................................

### What would make today great?

1. ...............................................................................................................................
2. ...............................................................................................................................
3. ...............................................................................................................................

## EVENING REFLECTION ●

I'm feeling:
...............................................................................................................................
...............................................................................................................................

### Great things that happened today

1. ...............................................................................................................................
2. ...............................................................................................................................
3. ...............................................................................................................................

Date:

## MORNING CHECK-IN ○

I'm feeling:

........................................................................................

........................................................................................

### Reasons to be grateful today

1. ...................................................................................

2. ...................................................................................

3. ...................................................................................

### What would make today great?

1. ...................................................................................

2. ...................................................................................

3. ...................................................................................

## EVENING REFLECTION ●

I'm feeling:

........................................................................................

........................................................................................

### Great things that happened today

1. ...................................................................................

2. ...................................................................................

3. ...................................................................................

Date:

## MORNING CHECK-IN ○

I'm feeling:

........................................................................................................................

........................................................................................................................

### Reasons to be grateful today

1.
........................................................................................................................

2.
........................................................................................................................

3.
........................................................................................................................

### What would make today great?

1.
........................................................................................................................

2.
........................................................................................................................

3.
........................................................................................................................

## EVENING REFLECTION ●

I'm feeling:

........................................................................................................................

........................................................................................................................

### Great things that happened today

1.
........................................................................................................................

2.
........................................................................................................................

3.
........................................................................................................................

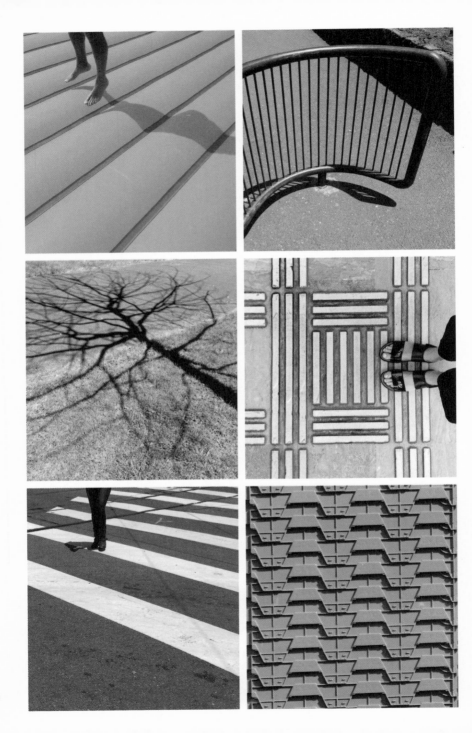

# Pattern Pondering No. 2
## Venturing Into the Unknown

Jumping on a trampoline with a friend, letting stripes lead you through a city, or taking a new route to work and noticing the tessellated tiles beneath your feet. Living life with more curiosity can lead us to joyful adventures each day. We'd love to see your own unexpected pattern explorations — share them with us @patternity.

"All are but parts of one stupendous whole."

Alexander Pope (1688–1744), English poet

Date:

## MORNING CHECK-IN  ○

I'm feeling:
...............................................................................................................
...............................................................................................................

### Reasons to be grateful today

1.
...............................................................................................................
2.
...............................................................................................................
3.
...............................................................................................................

### What would make today great?

1.
...............................................................................................................
2.
...............................................................................................................
3.
...............................................................................................................

## EVENING REFLECTION  ●

I'm feeling:
...............................................................................................................
...............................................................................................................

### Great things that happened today

1.
...............................................................................................................
2.
...............................................................................................................
3.
...............................................................................................................

Date:

## MORNING CHECK-IN ○

I'm feeling:
.................................................................................................

.................................................................................................

### Reasons to be grateful today

1. .............................................................................................
2. .............................................................................................
3. .............................................................................................

### What would make today great?

1. .............................................................................................
2. .............................................................................................
3. .............................................................................................

## EVENING REFLECTION ●

I'm feeling:
.................................................................................................

.................................................................................................

### Great things that happened today

1. .............................................................................................
2. .............................................................................................
3. .............................................................................................

Date:

## MORNING CHECK-IN ○

I'm feeling:
..........................................................................................................................
..........................................................................................................................

### Reasons to be grateful today

1. .......................................................................................................................
2. .......................................................................................................................
3. .......................................................................................................................

### What would make today great?

1. .......................................................................................................................
2. .......................................................................................................................
3. .......................................................................................................................

## EVENING REFLECTION ●

I'm feeling:
..........................................................................................................................
..........................................................................................................................

### Great things that happened today

1. .......................................................................................................................
2. .......................................................................................................................
3. .......................................................................................................................

Date:

## MORNING CHECK-IN       ○

I'm feeling:

..............................................................................................................................

..............................................................................................................................

### Reasons to be grateful today

1.
..............................................................................................................................
2.
..............................................................................................................................
3.
..............................................................................................................................

### What would make today great?

1.
..............................................................................................................................
2.
..............................................................................................................................
3.
..............................................................................................................................

## EVENING REFLECTION       ●

I'm feeling:

..............................................................................................................................

..............................................................................................................................

### Great things that happened today

1.
..............................................................................................................................
2.
..............................................................................................................................
3.
..............................................................................................................................

# Grateful Exploration No. 3

Inner Universe — Body Gratitude Scan | 20 minutes

## "The river is flowing. We are in it."

Richard Rohr (b. 1943), author

Many of us take our bodies and minds for granted. Instead of marveling at them as we might a spectacular galaxy or piece of art, we don't spend time getting to know, understand, and appreciate the wisdom and wonder of our own unique universe within, artfully working away to find balance and harmony as we go about our day-to-day lives.

Today take 20 minutes to systematically say thank you to your body for all the work it does for you.

## PREPARATION

Take a moment to find a comfortable position where you will be undisturbed, lying on your back with your arms slightly away from your body, palms up and feet relaxed, hip width apart.

First, bring your focus and awareness to your breathing, following the flow of the breath as it goes in through the nose and into the body, and again

as it leaves the body. Pause to prepare for the next inhale. Be grateful for this constant flow that gives you life.

Now bring your awareness to your feet and legs and down to your toes, thanking them for their daily support and the activities they allow you to do each day.

Bring your awareness up through the pelvis and torso; become aware of the bones in your hips, chest, and back that protect your vital organs. Notice the rise of your lungs, chest, and stomach expanding as you inhale, and now notice the fall as you exhale, sending oxygen around your body.

Now bring your awareness to your heart, noticing its gentle rhythms, the ceaseless pumping of blood around your body. Thank the heart as the center of your intuition; be grateful for the wisdom that it sends you every day. Take time and space to listen to its messages.

Now bring awareness to the other organs, the digestive system, the liver, the kidneys, all functioning together to feed and detoxify the body. Now bring awareness to the arms and

down to the hands; be grateful for the range of movement they allow us and everything they assist us with day to day.

Finally, bring your awareness up to the neck and to the head. Pause and take a moment to be grateful for each of your sensory organs — the mouth, the nose, the eyes, the ears — enjoy the sensory experiences of the world around you. Now go inside the head to the brain, its vast network of connections and impulses that allow us to plan, organize, remember, and pay attention.

Now feel the outside of your body, sensing the skin, your largest organ that keeps you protected and bridges the outer and inner world. And finally

feel your body as one entity; pause to thank it for working together as one system. Send it gratitude for its powers of collaboration, working ceaselessly, 24 hours a day, to help keep you healthy and alive.

## OBSERVATION

How did it make you feel? What came up?

Share your explorations on the free-flow pages at the back of the journal.

Visit us at patternity.org to find an audio recording of the Body Gratitude Scan

Date:

## MORNING CHECK-IN ○

I'm feeling:
..............................................................................................................
..............................................................................................................

### Reasons to be grateful today

1. ...........................................................................................................
2. ...........................................................................................................
3. ...........................................................................................................

### What would make today great?

1. ...........................................................................................................
2. ...........................................................................................................
3. ...........................................................................................................

## EVENING REFLECTION ●

I'm feeling:
..............................................................................................................
..............................................................................................................

### Great things that happened today

1. ...........................................................................................................
2. ...........................................................................................................
3. ...........................................................................................................

Date:

## MORNING CHECK-IN ○

I'm feeling:
........................................................................................
........................................................................................

### Reasons to be grateful today

1.
........................................................................................
2.
........................................................................................
3.
........................................................................................

### What would make today great?

1.
........................................................................................
2.
........................................................................................
3.
........................................................................................

## EVENING REFLECTION ●

I'm feeling:
........................................................................................
........................................................................................

### Great things that happened today

1.
........................................................................................
2.
........................................................................................
3.
........................................................................................

Date:

## MORNING CHECK-IN ○

I'm feeling:
..............................................................................................................................................

..............................................................................................................................................

### Reasons to be grateful today

1. ..........................................................................................................................................

2. ..........................................................................................................................................

3. ..........................................................................................................................................

### What would make today great?

1. ..........................................................................................................................................

2. ..........................................................................................................................................

3. ..........................................................................................................................................

## EVENING REFLECTION ●

I'm feeling:
..............................................................................................................................................

..............................................................................................................................................

### Great things that happened today

1. ..........................................................................................................................................

2. ..........................................................................................................................................

3. ..........................................................................................................................................

Date:

## MORNING CHECK-IN ○

I'm feeling:
............................................................................................................................
............................................................................................................................

### Reasons to be grateful today

1. ............................................................................................................................
2. ............................................................................................................................
3. ............................................................................................................................

### What would make today great?

1. ............................................................................................................................
2. ............................................................................................................................
3. ............................................................................................................................

## EVENING REFLECTION ●

I'm feeling:
............................................................................................................................
............................................................................................................................

### Great things that happened today

1. ............................................................................................................................
2. ............................................................................................................................
3. ............................................................................................................................

# VISUALIZE THE UNSEEN

Date:

## MORNING CHECK-IN ○

I'm feeling:
...................................................................................................
...................................................................................................

### Reasons to be grateful today

1. ...............................................................................................
2. ...............................................................................................
3. ...............................................................................................

### What would make today great?

1. ...............................................................................................
2. ...............................................................................................
3. ...............................................................................................

## EVENING REFLECTION ●

I'm feeling:
...................................................................................................
...................................................................................................

### Great things that happened today

1. ...............................................................................................
2. ...............................................................................................
3. ...............................................................................................

Date:

## MORNING CHECK-IN ○

I'm feeling:

.............................................................................................................................

.............................................................................................................................

### Reasons to be grateful today

1. .........................................................................................................................

2. .........................................................................................................................

3. .........................................................................................................................

### What would make today great?

1. .........................................................................................................................

2. .........................................................................................................................

3. .........................................................................................................................

## EVENING REFLECTION ●

I'm feeling:

.............................................................................................................................

.............................................................................................................................

### Great things that happened today

1. .........................................................................................................................

2. .........................................................................................................................

3. .........................................................................................................................

Date:

## MORNING CHECK-IN ○

I'm feeling:

........................................................................................

........................................................................................

### Reasons to be grateful today

1. ...............................................................................

2. ...............................................................................

3. ...............................................................................

### What would make today great?

1. ...............................................................................

2. ...............................................................................

3. ...............................................................................

## EVENING REFLECTION ●

I'm feeling:

........................................................................................

........................................................................................

### Great things that happened today

1. ...............................................................................

2. ...............................................................................

3. ...............................................................................

Date:

## MORNING CHECK-IN ○

I'm feeling:

................................................................................................

................................................................................................

### Reasons to be grateful today

1. ................................................................................................

2. ................................................................................................

3. ................................................................................................

### What would make today great?

1. ................................................................................................

2. ................................................................................................

3. ................................................................................................

## EVENING REFLECTION ●

I'm feeling:

................................................................................................

................................................................................................

### Great things that happened today

1. ................................................................................................

2. ................................................................................................

3. ................................................................................................

# Midpoint
# Celebration

Congratulations: you are
halfway through the journal.

This week, take 30 minutes out of your schedule to celebrate your personal progress. Simply do something nourishing, relaxing, and joyful for you.

Be grateful to yourself for doing the work so far.

Enjoy!

Date:

## MORNING CHECK-IN ○

I'm feeling:
............................................................................................................

............................................................................................................

### Reasons to be grateful today

1. ............................................................................................................
2. ............................................................................................................
3. ............................................................................................................

### What would make today great?

1. ............................................................................................................
2. ............................................................................................................
3. ............................................................................................................

## EVENING REFLECTION ●

I'm feeling:
............................................................................................................

............................................................................................................

### Great things that happened today

1. ............................................................................................................
2. ............................................................................................................
3. ............................................................................................................

Date:

## MORNING CHECK-IN ○

I'm feeling:
...............................................................................................................................................
...............................................................................................................................................

### Reasons to be grateful today

1.
...............................................................................................................................................
2.
...............................................................................................................................................
3.
...............................................................................................................................................

### What would make today great?

1.
...............................................................................................................................................
2.
...............................................................................................................................................
3.
...............................................................................................................................................

## EVENING REFLECTION ●

I'm feeling:
...............................................................................................................................................
...............................................................................................................................................

### Great things that happened today

1.
...............................................................................................................................................
2.
...............................................................................................................................................
3.
...............................................................................................................................................

Date:

## MORNING CHECK-IN  ○

I'm feeling:
.................................................................................................................................
.................................................................................................................................

### Reasons to be grateful today

1. ..............................................................................................................................
2. ..............................................................................................................................
3. ..............................................................................................................................

### What would make today great?

1. ..............................................................................................................................
2. ..............................................................................................................................
3. ..............................................................................................................................

## EVENING REFLECTION  ●

I'm feeling:
.................................................................................................................................
.................................................................................................................................

### Great things that happened today

1. ..............................................................................................................................
2. ..............................................................................................................................
3. ..............................................................................................................................

# Pause + Reflect

## Heartbeats

Our bodies are constantly adapting to and harmonizing with the world around us. Your heartbeat even changes and mimics the music and sounds you listen to. We are often so bombarded by sounds that we underappreciate how beautifully sensitive our bodies are. Today try listening to your favorite song with your whole being. How did it make you feel? If you could visualize it, what shape or pattern would it be? Perhaps try exploring this visually on your free-flow pages.

Date:

## MORNING CHECK-IN $\bigcirc$

I'm feeling:
...............................................................................................

...............................................................................................

### Reasons to be grateful today

1. ...........................................................................................

2. ...........................................................................................

3. ...........................................................................................

### What would make today great?

1. ...........................................................................................

2. ...........................................................................................

3. ...........................................................................................


## EVENING REFLECTION ●

I'm feeling:
...............................................................................................

...............................................................................................

### Great things that happened today

1. ...........................................................................................

2. ...........................................................................................

3. ...........................................................................................

Date:

## MORNING CHECK-IN      ○

I'm feeling:
.........................................................................................................................................

.........................................................................................................................................

### Reasons to be grateful today

1.
.........................................................................................................................................
2.
.........................................................................................................................................
3.
.........................................................................................................................................

### What would make today great?

1.
.........................................................................................................................................
2.
.........................................................................................................................................
3.
.........................................................................................................................................

## EVENING REFLECTION      ●

I'm feeling:
.........................................................................................................................................

.........................................................................................................................................

### Great things that happened today

1.
.........................................................................................................................................
2.
.........................................................................................................................................
3.
.........................................................................................................................................

Date:

## MORNING CHECK-IN ○

I'm feeling:
.......................................................................................................................................

.......................................................................................................................................

### Reasons to be grateful today

1. ...............................................................................................................................

2. ...............................................................................................................................

3. ...............................................................................................................................

### What would make today great?

1. ...............................................................................................................................

2. ...............................................................................................................................

3. ...............................................................................................................................

## EVENING REFLECTION ●

I'm feeling:
.......................................................................................................................................

.......................................................................................................................................

### Great things that happened today

1. ...............................................................................................................................

2. ...............................................................................................................................

3. ...............................................................................................................................

Date:

## MORNING CHECK-IN    ○

I'm feeling:

.......................................................................................................

.......................................................................................................


### Reasons to be grateful today

1. ...................................................................................................

2. ...................................................................................................

3. ...................................................................................................


### What would make today great?

1. ...................................................................................................

2. ...................................................................................................

3. ...................................................................................................

## EVENING REFLECTION    ●

I'm feeling:

.......................................................................................................

.......................................................................................................


### Great things that happened today

1. ...................................................................................................

2. ...................................................................................................

3. ...................................................................................................

# DIG
# BENEATH
# THE
# SURFACE

Date:

## MORNING CHECK-IN ○

I'm feeling:
......................................................................................................

......................................................................................................

### Reasons to be grateful today

1. ....................................................................................................
2. ....................................................................................................
3. ....................................................................................................

### What would make today great?

1. ....................................................................................................
2. ....................................................................................................
3. ....................................................................................................

## EVENING REFLECTION ●

I'm feeling:
......................................................................................................

......................................................................................................

### Great things that happened today

1. ....................................................................................................
2. ....................................................................................................
3. ....................................................................................................

Date:

## MORNING CHECK-IN ○

I'm feeling:
.............................................................................................
.............................................................................................

### Reasons to be grateful today

1.
.............................................................................................
2.
.............................................................................................
3.
.............................................................................................

### What would make today great?

1.
.............................................................................................
2.
.............................................................................................
3.
.............................................................................................

## EVENING REFLECTION ●

I'm feeling:
.............................................................................................
.............................................................................................

### Great things that happened today

1.
.............................................................................................
2.
.............................................................................................
3.
.............................................................................................

Date:

## MORNING CHECK-IN ○

I'm feeling:

......................................................................................................................

......................................................................................................................

### Reasons to be grateful today

1. ...............................................................................................................

2. ...............................................................................................................

3. ...............................................................................................................

### What would make today great?

1. ...............................................................................................................

2. ...............................................................................................................

3. ...............................................................................................................


## EVENING REFLECTION ●

I'm feeling:

......................................................................................................................

......................................................................................................................

### Great things that happened today

1. ...............................................................................................................

2. ...............................................................................................................

3. ...............................................................................................................

Date:

## MORNING CHECK-IN  ○

I'm feeling:
..................................................................................................................................................

..................................................................................................................................................

### Reasons to be grateful today

1.
..................................................................................................................................................
2.
..................................................................................................................................................
3.
..................................................................................................................................................

### What would make today great?

1.
..................................................................................................................................................
2.
..................................................................................................................................................
3.
..................................................................................................................................................

## EVENING REFLECTION  ●

I'm feeling:
..................................................................................................................................................

..................................................................................................................................................

### Great things that happened today

1.
..................................................................................................................................................
2.
..................................................................................................................................................
3.
..................................................................................................................................................

# Grateful Exploration No. 4

Embrace the Negative — Growth Chart | 30 minutes

"All things are filled full of signs, and it is a wise man who can learn about one thing from another."

Plotinus (AD 205–270), Roman Neoplatonist philosopher

It can be easy to foster gratitude when life is flowing as we want it to, but how about when it isn't? Often in the effort of trying to avoid or push away the more difficult experiences, feelings, or emotions in life, we miss valuable opportunities to learn and grow. Digging deeper in times of difficulty can make us more resilient as we learn how to adapt and take on future challenges.

## PREPARATION

Think of a difficult time in your life — an occasion when you've had a hard experience with something or someone — and how it's turned out to be something positive in the end. What qualities or techniques did you put into action? Perhaps you made a new discovery about yourself, created a change of direction, or made a new connection?

## OBSERVATION

Describe your difficult experience in a stream of consciousness. Don't think too much about it; just put pen to page. Let the words flow as a stream of words without judgment or critique.

How did it make you feel?

How do you feel about it now?

What did you learn from that experience?

Can you feel grateful to the experience for having shaped you?

Explore this further in the free-flow pages at the back of your journal

Date:

## MORNING CHECK-IN ○

I'm feeling:

.................................................................................................

.................................................................................................

### Reasons to be grateful today

1. .............................................................................................
2. .............................................................................................
3. .............................................................................................

### What would make today great?

1. .............................................................................................
2. .............................................................................................
3. .............................................................................................

## EVENING REFLECTION ●

I'm feeling:

.................................................................................................

.................................................................................................

### Great things that happened today

1. .............................................................................................
2. .............................................................................................
3. .............................................................................................

Date:

## MORNING CHECK-IN ○

I'm feeling:
.......................................................................................

.......................................................................................

### Reasons to be grateful today

1. ....................................................................................
2. ....................................................................................
3. ....................................................................................

### What would make today great?

1. ....................................................................................
2. ....................................................................................
3. ....................................................................................

## EVENING REFLECTION ●

I'm feeling:
.......................................................................................

.......................................................................................

### Great things that happened today

1. ....................................................................................
2. ....................................................................................
3. ....................................................................................

( II )

# Pause + Reflect

## Laughter Log

Research has shown that in addition to boosting mood, laughing regularly can improve immunity, help regulate blood flow, and improve our sleep patterns. When was the last time something made you laugh out loud? Start a laughter log noticing the moments that sparked joy for you this week and writing them down. What were the commonalities? Consider ways in which you can invite more laughter and lightness into your day-to-day life.

Date:

## MORNING CHECK-IN ○

I'm feeling:

......................................................................................................................

......................................................................................................................

### Reasons to be grateful today

1. ...............................................................................................................

2. ...............................................................................................................

3. ...............................................................................................................

### What would make today great?

1. ...............................................................................................................

2. ...............................................................................................................

3. ...............................................................................................................

## EVENING REFLECTION ●

I'm feeling:

......................................................................................................................

......................................................................................................................

### Great things that happened today

1. ...............................................................................................................

2. ...............................................................................................................

3. ...............................................................................................................

Date:

## MORNING CHECK-IN ○

I'm feeling:
...................................................................................................
...................................................................................................

### Reasons to be grateful today

1.
...................................................................................................
2.
...................................................................................................
3.
...................................................................................................

### What would make today great?

1.
...................................................................................................
2.
...................................................................................................
3.
...................................................................................................

## EVENING REFLECTION ●

I'm feeling:
...................................................................................................
...................................................................................................

### Great things that happened today

1.
...................................................................................................
2.
...................................................................................................
3.
...................................................................................................

Date:

## MORNING CHECK-IN ○

I'm feeling:
..........................................................................................................
..........................................................................................................

### Reasons to be grateful today

1. ..........................................................................................................
2. ..........................................................................................................
3. ..........................................................................................................

### What would make today great?

1. ..........................................................................................................
2. ..........................................................................................................
3. ..........................................................................................................

## EVENING REFLECTION ●

I'm feeling:
..........................................................................................................
..........................................................................................................

### Great things that happened today

1. ..........................................................................................................
2. ..........................................................................................................
3. ..........................................................................................................

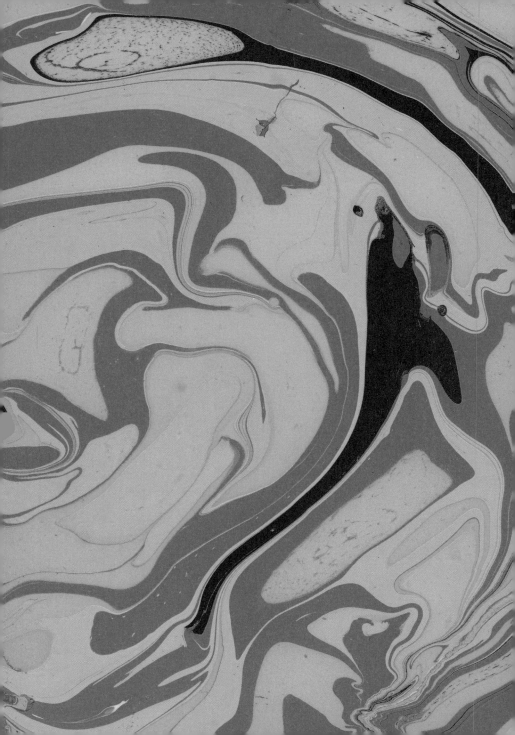

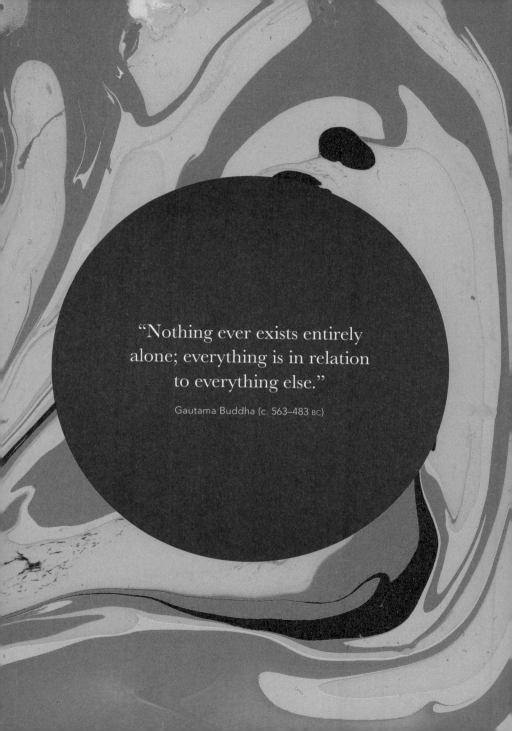

"Nothing ever exists entirely alone; everything is in relation to everything else."

Gautama Buddha (c. 563–483 BC)

# Magnificent

## Exploring the Wonder + Joy of Interconnectivity

Having looked deep within ourselves, it's now time to zoom outward. Far outward ... It wasn't until astronauts were looking back at Earth from space that they were able to find a new perspective that highlighted the fragile interrelatedness of our collective home. In a world where so many systems and structures seem to be falling out of balance, this chapter looks to find simple ways to inspire a deeper sense of wonder and a hopeful connection to a much greater whole that puts purpose and giving at the heart of living each day.

Date:

## MORNING CHECK-IN ○

I'm feeling:

...................................................................................................................

...................................................................................................................

### Reasons to be grateful today

1. ...............................................................................................................

2. ...............................................................................................................

3. ...............................................................................................................

### What would make today great?

1. ...............................................................................................................

2. ...............................................................................................................

3. ...............................................................................................................

## EVENING REFLECTION ●

I'm feeling:

...................................................................................................................

...................................................................................................................

### Great things that happened today

1. ...............................................................................................................

2. ...............................................................................................................

3. ...............................................................................................................

Date:

## MORNING CHECK-IN  ○

I'm feeling:
..........................................................................................................................................................

..........................................................................................................................................................

### Reasons to be grateful today

1. ........................................................................................................................................................

2. ........................................................................................................................................................

3. ........................................................................................................................................................

### What would make today great?

1. ........................................................................................................................................................

2. ........................................................................................................................................................

3. ........................................................................................................................................................

## EVENING REFLECTION  ●

I'm feeling:
..........................................................................................................................................................

..........................................................................................................................................................

### Great things that happened today

1. ........................................................................................................................................................

2. ........................................................................................................................................................

3. ........................................................................................................................................................

Date:

## MORNING CHECK-IN  ◯

I'm feeling:

................................................................

................................................................

### Reasons to be grateful today

1. ................................................................

2. ................................................................

3. ................................................................

### What would make today great?

1. ................................................................

2. ................................................................

3. ................................................................

## EVENING REFLECTION  ●

I'm feeling:

................................................................

................................................................

### Great things that happened today

1. ................................................................

2. ................................................................

3. ................................................................

Date:

## MORNING CHECK-IN ○

I'm feeling:
..............................................................................................................................
..............................................................................................................................

### Reasons to be grateful today

1.
..............................................................................................................................
2.
..............................................................................................................................
3.
..............................................................................................................................

### What would make today great?

1.
..............................................................................................................................
2.
..............................................................................................................................
3.
..............................................................................................................................

## EVENING REFLECTION ●

I'm feeling:
..............................................................................................................................
..............................................................................................................................

### Great things that happened today

1.
..............................................................................................................................
2.
..............................................................................................................................
3.
..............................................................................................................................

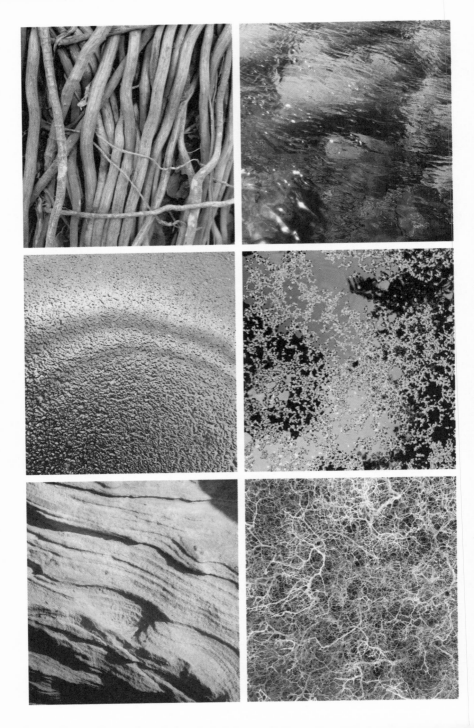

# Pattern Pondering No. 3

## Sensing the Bigger Picture

Ponder the ripples of water that resonate with our own brain waves, or appreciate the roots that dig deep into the soil below our feet so we can breathe fresh air. Taking time to ponder the invisible connections of which we are a part can be humbling, helping us feel more unified with the planet that supports and nourishes us all daily. Take some time to stare into space and share your pattern ponderings with us @patternity.

> "The goal of life is living in agreement with nature."

Zeno of Elea (c. 490–430 BC), Greek philosopher

Date:

## MORNING CHECK-IN ○

I'm feeling:
...........................................................................................................................
...........................................................................................................................

### Reasons to be grateful today

1. ..........................................................................................................
2. ..........................................................................................................
3. ..........................................................................................................

### What would make today great?

1. ..........................................................................................................
2. ..........................................................................................................
3. ..........................................................................................................

## EVENING REFLECTION ●

I'm feeling:
...........................................................................................................................
...........................................................................................................................

### Great things that happened today

1. ..........................................................................................................
2. ..........................................................................................................
3. ..........................................................................................................

Date:

## MORNING CHECK-IN ◯

I'm feeling:

.................................................................................................................

.................................................................................................................

### Reasons to be grateful today

1.
.................................................................................................................
2.
.................................................................................................................
3.
.................................................................................................................

### What would make today great?

1.
.................................................................................................................
2.
.................................................................................................................
3.
.................................................................................................................

## EVENING REFLECTION ●

I'm feeling:

.................................................................................................................

.................................................................................................................

### Great things that happened today

1.
.................................................................................................................
2.
.................................................................................................................
3.
.................................................................................................................

Date:

## MORNING CHECK-IN ○

I'm feeling:
..........................................................................................
..........................................................................................

### Reasons to be grateful today

1. ...................................................................................
2. ...................................................................................
3. ...................................................................................

### What would make today great?

1. ...................................................................................
2. ...................................................................................
3. ...................................................................................

## EVENING REFLECTION ●

I'm feeling:
..........................................................................................
..........................................................................................

### Great things that happened today

1. ...................................................................................
2. ...................................................................................
3. ...................................................................................

Date:

## MORNING CHECK-IN ○

I'm feeling:

.........................................................................................................

.........................................................................................................

### Reasons to be grateful today

1.
.........................................................................................................
2.
.........................................................................................................
3.
.........................................................................................................

### What would make today great?

1.
.........................................................................................................
2.
.........................................................................................................
3.
.........................................................................................................

## EVENING REFLECTION ●

I'm feeling:

.........................................................................................................

.........................................................................................................

### Great things that happened today

1.
.........................................................................................................
2.
.........................................................................................................
3.
.........................................................................................................

# Grateful Exploration No. 5

Relationship Reciprocity — The Me Tree | 1 hour

## "Nature is not a place to visit. It is home."

Gary Snyder (b. 1930), poet

Not only are trees essential for life, but as the longest living species on Earth, they give us a link between the past, present, and future. But how can the relationships between trees and their environment inspire us in our own lives? Taking a tree as a metaphor, try exploring the following experiment.

There is no right or wrong way to create your me tree; let the words flow and find their own path.

### ROOTS: NOURISHMENT

What are my best qualities, beliefs? What am I most proud of in myself? What foundations ground me?

### TRUNK: SUPPORT

What places, people, and perspectives help me to feel strong, solid, and supported?

### BRANCHES: CONNECTIONS

Who am I connected to or who would I like to be connected to in order to branch wide and blossom? What individuals, organizations, or wider networks would I like to connect to?

### LEAVES: GIVING BACK

What are my gifts? What talents, qualities, and actions do I want to give out and back to the world? What do I want to be remembered for as the results of my actions fall back to Earth and nourish the system?

Share your images of bark, branches, and leaves with us via @patternity #BeGreatBeGrateful

Date:

## MORNING CHECK-IN ○

I'm feeling:
...................................................................................................................
...................................................................................................................

### Reasons to be grateful today

1. ..............................................................................................................
2. ..............................................................................................................
3. ..............................................................................................................

### What would make today great?

1. ..............................................................................................................
2. ..............................................................................................................
3. ..............................................................................................................

## EVENING REFLECTION ●

I'm feeling:
...................................................................................................................
...................................................................................................................

### Great things that happened today

1. ..............................................................................................................
2. ..............................................................................................................
3. ..............................................................................................................

Date:

## MORNING CHECK-IN ○

I'm feeling:

........................................................................

........................................................................

### Reasons to be grateful today

1. ...............................................................
2. ...............................................................
3. ...............................................................

### What would make today great?

1. ...............................................................
2. ...............................................................
3. ...............................................................

## EVENING REFLECTION ●

I'm feeling:

........................................................................

........................................................................

### Great things that happened today

1. ...............................................................
2. ...............................................................
3. ...............................................................

Date:

## MORNING CHECK-IN     ◯

I'm feeling:
..............................................................................................................................
..............................................................................................................................

### Reasons to be grateful today

1. ...........................................................................................................................
2. ...........................................................................................................................
3. ...........................................................................................................................

### What would make today great?

1. ...........................................................................................................................
2. ...........................................................................................................................
3. ...........................................................................................................................

## EVENING REFLECTION     ●

I'm feeling:
..............................................................................................................................
..............................................................................................................................

### Great things that happened today

1. ...........................................................................................................................
2. ...........................................................................................................................
3. ...........................................................................................................................

Date:

## MORNING CHECK-IN ○

I'm feeling:

.........................................................................................

.........................................................................................

### Reasons to be grateful today

1. ...................................................................................

2. ...................................................................................

3. ...................................................................................

### What would make today great?

1. ...................................................................................

2. ...................................................................................

3. ...................................................................................

## EVENING REFLECTION ●

I'm feeling:

.........................................................................................

.........................................................................................

### Great things that happened today

1. ...................................................................................

2. ...................................................................................

3. ...................................................................................

# CELEBRATE CONNECTIVITY

Date:

## MORNING CHECK-IN   ○

I'm feeling:
...........................................................................................................
...........................................................................................................

### Reasons to be grateful today

1. ........................................................................................................
2. ........................................................................................................
3. ........................................................................................................

### What would make today great?

1. ........................................................................................................
2. ........................................................................................................
3. ........................................................................................................

## EVENING REFLECTION   ●

I'm feeling:
...........................................................................................................
...........................................................................................................

### Great things that happened today

1. ........................................................................................................
2. ........................................................................................................
3. ........................................................................................................

Date:

## MORNING CHECK-IN ○

I'm feeling:
...............................................................................................................................
...............................................................................................................................

### Reasons to be grateful today

1.
...............................................................................................................................
2.
...............................................................................................................................
3.
...............................................................................................................................

### What would make today great?

1.
...............................................................................................................................
2.
...............................................................................................................................
3.
...............................................................................................................................

## EVENING REFLECTION ●

I'm feeling:
...............................................................................................................................
...............................................................................................................................

### Great things that happened today

1.
...............................................................................................................................
2.
...............................................................................................................................
3.
...............................................................................................................................

Date:

## MORNING CHECK-IN ◯

I'm feeling:
..............................................................................................................
..............................................................................................................

### Reasons to be grateful today

1. .........................................................................................................
2. .........................................................................................................
3. .........................................................................................................

### What would make today great?

1. .........................................................................................................
2. .........................................................................................................
3. .........................................................................................................

## EVENING REFLECTION ●

I'm feeling:
..............................................................................................................
..............................................................................................................

### Great things that happened today

1. .........................................................................................................
2. .........................................................................................................
3. .........................................................................................................

# Pause + Reflect

## Ancestors

Our individual experience of today is the result of an infinite web of invisible threads and actions that extend as far back into time as we can imagine. Spend a few moments remembering a friend, colleague, family member, or cultural figure who you are really grateful for. Someone who has inspired or shaped your life journey in some way. Consider doing something good for someone else in their honor today.

Date:

## MORNING CHECK-IN ○

I'm feeling:

........................................................................................

........................................................................................

### Reasons to be grateful today

1. ........................................................................................
2. ........................................................................................
3. ........................................................................................

### What would make today great?

1. ........................................................................................
2. ........................................................................................
3. ........................................................................................

## EVENING REFLECTION ●

I'm feeling:

........................................................................................

........................................................................................

### Great things that happened today

1. ........................................................................................
2. ........................................................................................
3. ........................................................................................

Date:

## MORNING CHECK-IN                    ○

I'm feeling:

.............................................................................................................

.............................................................................................................

### Reasons to be grateful today

1.
.............................................................................................................
2.
.............................................................................................................
3.
.............................................................................................................

### What would make today great?

1.
.............................................................................................................
2.
.............................................................................................................
3.
.............................................................................................................

## EVENING REFLECTION                    ●

I'm feeling:

.............................................................................................................

.............................................................................................................

### Great things that happened today

1.
.............................................................................................................
2.
.............................................................................................................
3.
.............................................................................................................

Date:

## MORNING CHECK-IN ○

I'm feeling:
................................................................................................
................................................................................................

### Reasons to be grateful today

1. ............................................................................................
2. ............................................................................................
3. ............................................................................................

### What would make today great?

1. ............................................................................................
2. ............................................................................................
3. ............................................................................................

## EVENING REFLECTION ●

I'm feeling:
................................................................................................
................................................................................................

### Great things that happened today

1. ............................................................................................
2. ............................................................................................
3. ............................................................................................

Date:

## MORNING CHECK-IN ○

I'm feeling:

........................................................................................

........................................................................................

### Reasons to be grateful today

1. ........................................................................................
2. ........................................................................................
3. ........................................................................................

### What would make today great?

1. ........................................................................................
2. ........................................................................................
3. ........................................................................................

## EVENING REFLECTION ●

I'm feeling:

........................................................................................

........................................................................................

### Great things that happened today

1. ........................................................................................
2. ........................................................................................
3. ........................................................................................

# TO LIVE
# IS TO GIVE

Date:

## MORNING CHECK-IN ○

I'm feeling:

.....................................................................................................................

.....................................................................................................................

### Reasons to be grateful today

1. .................................................................................................................

2. .................................................................................................................

3. .................................................................................................................

### What would make today great?

1. .................................................................................................................

2. .................................................................................................................

3. .................................................................................................................

## EVENING REFLECTION ●

I'm feeling:

.....................................................................................................................

.....................................................................................................................

### Great things that happened today

1. .................................................................................................................

2. .................................................................................................................

3. .................................................................................................................

Date:

## MORNING CHECK-IN  ○

I'm feeling:
...................................................................................................................

...................................................................................................................

### Reasons to be grateful today

1. ...............................................................................................................
2. ...............................................................................................................
3. ...............................................................................................................

### What would make today great?

1. ...............................................................................................................
2. ...............................................................................................................
3. ...............................................................................................................

## EVENING REFLECTION  ●

I'm feeling:
...................................................................................................................

...................................................................................................................

### Great things that happened today

1. ...............................................................................................................
2. ...............................................................................................................
3. ...............................................................................................................

Date:

## MORNING CHECK-IN ○

I'm feeling:

......................................................................................................................

......................................................................................................................

### Reasons to be grateful today

1. .................................................................................................................

2. .................................................................................................................

3. .................................................................................................................

### What would make today great?

1. .................................................................................................................

2. .................................................................................................................

3. .................................................................................................................

## EVENING REFLECTION ●

I'm feeling:

......................................................................................................................

......................................................................................................................

### Great things that happened today

1. .................................................................................................................

2. .................................................................................................................

3. .................................................................................................................

Date:

## MORNING CHECK-IN ○

I'm feeling:

.........................................................................................

.........................................................................................

### Reasons to be grateful today

1. .......................................................................................

2. .......................................................................................

3. .......................................................................................

### What would make today great?

1. .......................................................................................

2. .......................................................................................

3. .......................................................................................

## EVENING REFLECTION ●

I'm feeling:

.........................................................................................

.........................................................................................

### Great things that happened today

1. .......................................................................................

2. .......................................................................................

3. .......................................................................................

# Grateful Exploration No. 6

Nature and Me — Wild Solo | 1 hour to 1 day

"If you go off into a far, far forest and get very quiet, you'll come to understand that you're connected to everything."

Alan Watts (1915–1973), philosopher

Time spent in nature has countless benefits for the wellbeing of both our body and our mind — reduced stress, increased self-esteem, and emotional balance. In an increasingly complex culture, our basic dependency on the air, sun, earth, and the rain has faded into the background, and the tender relationships between plants, animals, and all living things lie largely out of view.

This week, prepare to take some time out of your schedule to venture into nature for some solitude and reconnection with the system that gently and silently supports us all each day.

## PREPARATION

Think of a spot in nature that you feel a positive connection with — somewhere that is safe and where you are unlikely to be disturbed (the park, woodland).

Pack appropriate clothes, food, and water to keep you comfortable for your chosen solo duration. Also take a watch, notepad, and a pen.

Remember to disconnect all your electronic devices.

Find a place you are particularly drawn to and would feel comfortable sitting down in for at least an hour.

Take a moment to ground yourself, taking in the smells, sounds, sights, and textures around you. Take a moment to connect with the sky above your head and the earth beneath your feet. If it's not too cold, remove your shoes to connect with the earth.

Let your surroundings and curiosity lead you in the direction you would like to take for your solo time.

When you settle into your spot, take a few moments to thank the earth beneath you and whatever is above you for supporting and protecting you

as you take the time to connect with your environment.

For the remaining time of your solo adventure, use all of your senses to soak in the world around you, both up close and far away. Look closely at textures and details. How have the elements affected your surroundings? Are things dying? Coming to life? What cycles and relationships can you see?

Notice how you notice things. What are you drawn to? Be curious about your own senses and intuition.

More than anything, see if you can let go of aims and outcomes. See if you can just allow life to flow.

When your timer sounds, gently come back to yourself and take a moment to thank yourself for taking the time

and commitment to connect with nature — and yourself. This is a good time to switch off your devices and simply end the exploration when the time feels right for you.

Over the next few days, write down some personal reflections on what came up for you during this time. Give yourself space to relax and let your thoughts emerge.

A special thanks to Way of Nature for guiding us on our own wild solo adventure.

Write to us about your explorations at studio@patternity.org so we can share them

Date:

## MORNING CHECK-IN ○

I'm feeling:

......................................................................................................................................

......................................................................................................................................

### Reasons to be grateful today

1. ..............................................................................................................................

2. ..............................................................................................................................

3. ..............................................................................................................................

### What would make today great?

1. ..............................................................................................................................

2. ..............................................................................................................................

3. ..............................................................................................................................

## EVENING REFLECTION ●

I'm feeling:

......................................................................................................................................

......................................................................................................................................

### Great things that happened today

1. ..............................................................................................................................

2. ..............................................................................................................................

3. ..............................................................................................................................

Date:

## MORNING CHECK-IN        ○

I'm feeling:

....................................................................................................

....................................................................................................

### Reasons to be grateful today

1.
....................................................................................................
2.
....................................................................................................
3.
....................................................................................................

### What would make today great?

1.
....................................................................................................
2.
....................................................................................................
3.
....................................................................................................

## EVENING REFLECTION        ●

I'm feeling:

....................................................................................................

....................................................................................................

### Great things that happened today

1.
....................................................................................................
2.
....................................................................................................
3.
....................................................................................................

Date:

## MORNING CHECK-IN ○

I'm feeling:

......................................................................................................

......................................................................................................

### Reasons to be grateful today

1. ...............................................................................................
2. ...............................................................................................
3. ...............................................................................................

### What would make today great?

1. ...............................................................................................
2. ...............................................................................................
3. ...............................................................................................

## EVENING REFLECTION ●

I'm feeling:

......................................................................................................

......................................................................................................

### Great things that happened today

1. ...............................................................................................
2. ...............................................................................................
3. ...............................................................................................

Date:

## MORNING CHECK-IN ○

I'm feeling:

........................................................................................................................................

........................................................................................................................................

### Reasons to be grateful today

1.
........................................................................................................................................
2.
........................................................................................................................................
3.
........................................................................................................................................

### What would make today great?

1.
........................................................................................................................................
2.
........................................................................................................................................
3.
........................................................................................................................................

## EVENING REFLECTION ●

I'm feeling:

........................................................................................................................................

........................................................................................................................................

### Great things that happened today

1.
........................................................................................................................................
2.
........................................................................................................................................
3.
........................................................................................................................................

# Pause + Reflect

## Cosmic Connections

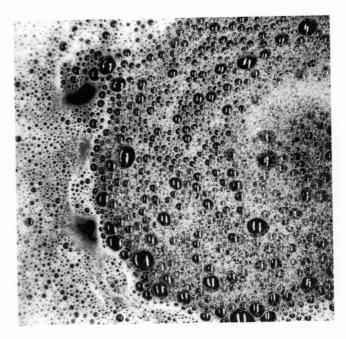

Our ancient ancestors' reverence for the sun, moon, and stars was woven into their culture, forming much of their understanding of the cyclic nature of life on Earth. In an increasingly individualistic age, reflecting on the awesome vastness of space and our connection to an infinite celestial system can put our daily concerns into perspective. On the next clear night, try looking up to appreciate the 13.772 billion years of evolution that have allowed for life here in this solar system.

Date:

## MORNING CHECK-IN ○

I'm feeling:
..............................................................................................................................................
..............................................................................................................................................

### Reasons to be grateful today

1. ........................................................................................................................................
2. ........................................................................................................................................
3. ........................................................................................................................................

### What would make today great?

1. ........................................................................................................................................
2. ........................................................................................................................................
3. ........................................................................................................................................

## EVENING REFLECTION ●

I'm feeling:
..............................................................................................................................................
..............................................................................................................................................

### Great things that happened today

1. ........................................................................................................................................
2. ........................................................................................................................................
3. ........................................................................................................................................

Date:

## MORNING CHECK-IN ○

I'm feeling:

......................................................................................................................

......................................................................................................................

### Reasons to be grateful today

1. ...............................................................................................................
2. ...............................................................................................................
3. ...............................................................................................................

### What would make today great?

1. ...............................................................................................................
2. ...............................................................................................................
3. ...............................................................................................................

## EVENING REFLECTION ●

I'm feeling:

......................................................................................................................

......................................................................................................................

### Great things that happened today

1. ...............................................................................................................
2. ...............................................................................................................
3. ...............................................................................................................

Date:

## MORNING CHECK-IN  ○

I'm feeling:

...................................................................................................................

...................................................................................................................

### Reasons to be grateful today

1. ...............................................................................................................

2. ...............................................................................................................

3. ...............................................................................................................

### What would make today great?

1. ...............................................................................................................

2. ...............................................................................................................

3. ...............................................................................................................

## EVENING REFLECTION  ●

I'm feeling:

...................................................................................................................

...................................................................................................................

### Great things that happened today

1. ...............................................................................................................

2. ...............................................................................................................

3. ...............................................................................................................

Date:

## MORNING CHECK-IN  ○

I'm feeling:

........................................................................................

........................................................................................

### Reasons to be grateful today

1. ..................................................................................
2. ..................................................................................
3. ..................................................................................

### What would make today great?

1. ..................................................................................
2. ..................................................................................
3. ..................................................................................

## EVENING REFLECTION  ●

I'm feeling:

........................................................................................

........................................................................................

### Great things that happened today

1. ..................................................................................
2. ..................................................................................
3. ..................................................................................

# Pause + Reflect

## Supply Cycles

In a world of abundance it's easy to forget how much time, effort, and energy goes into making even the humblest product on the supermarket shelf. Take a moment to think of one of your favorite products that you love and enjoy, from nectarines to newspapers. Imagine the web of people, processes, and places involved in making it. Send some gratitude out to the supply chain next time you enjoy it.

Date:

## MORNING CHECK-IN ○

I'm feeling:
.............................................................................................................
.............................................................................................................

### Reasons to be grateful today

1. ..........................................................................................................
2. ..........................................................................................................
3. ..........................................................................................................

### What would make today great?

1. ..........................................................................................................
2. ..........................................................................................................
3. ..........................................................................................................

## EVENING REFLECTION ●

I'm feeling:
.............................................................................................................
.............................................................................................................

### Great things that happened today

1. ..........................................................................................................
2. ..........................................................................................................
3. ..........................................................................................................

Date:

## MORNING CHECK-IN ○

I'm feeling:
..........................................................................................................................
..........................................................................................................................

### Reasons to be grateful today

1. ........................................................................................................................
2. ........................................................................................................................
3. ........................................................................................................................

### What would make today great?

1. ........................................................................................................................
2. ........................................................................................................................
3. ........................................................................................................................

## EVENING REFLECTION ●

I'm feeling:
..........................................................................................................................
..........................................................................................................................

### Great things that happened today

1. ........................................................................................................................
2. ........................................................................................................................
3. ........................................................................................................................

Date:

## MORNING CHECK-IN ○

I'm feeling:

..........................................................................................................

..........................................................................................................

### Reasons to be grateful today

1. .......................................................................................................

2. .......................................................................................................

3. .......................................................................................................

### What would make today great?

1. .......................................................................................................

2. .......................................................................................................

3. .......................................................................................................

## EVENING REFLECTION ●

I'm feeling:

..........................................................................................................

..........................................................................................................

### Great things that happened today

1. .......................................................................................................

2. .......................................................................................................

3. .......................................................................................................

Date:

## MORNING CHECK-IN ○

I'm feeling:
..........................................................................................................................................

..........................................................................................................................................

### Reasons to be grateful today

1. ......................................................................................................................................

2. ......................................................................................................................................

3. ......................................................................................................................................

### What would make today great?

1. ......................................................................................................................................

2. ......................................................................................................................................

3. ......................................................................................................................................

## EVENING REFLECTION ●

I'm feeling:
..........................................................................................................................................

..........................................................................................................................................

### Great things that happened today

1. ......................................................................................................................................

2. ......................................................................................................................................

3. ......................................................................................................................................

# Check-Out

## Reviewing Your Personal Pattern

You've now reached the end of the gratitude journal. We hope you've enjoyed the journey and that it has inspired some positive patterns. As we move into the last few pages of the journal, take stock of your journey so far.

- What went well and what didn't?
- What were the biggest challenges?
- How did you grow throughout the pages?
- What were the most meaningful moments?
- What insights served you best?
- Will you be continuing your own grateful pages?

Fill in the personal pattern and compare it to the one you made at the beginning — has anything changed? How does this make you feel? What's come up for you while reflecting on your personal pattern?

Share your experience with
us at studio@patternity.org

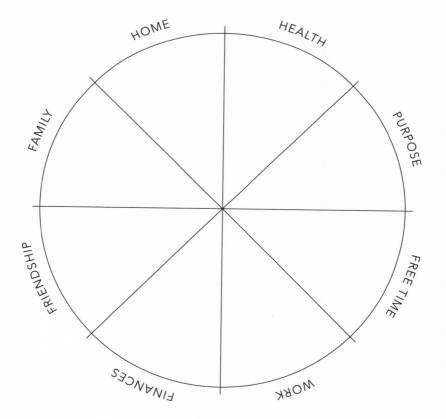

# Continue Your Grateful Journey

"If you want to go fast, go alone.
If you want to go far, go together."

African proverb

We hope you found your grateful journal inspiring and empowering. If you'd like to get involved further — whether with a future pattern-focused event; to suggest a project, contribute your ideas, or take part in one of our future experiences; or to share any of your thoughts, feelings, or explorations from your own grateful journey — we'd love to hear from you.

# With Gratitude

Whether you've joined us at an event, given us some advice, commissioned us on a project, or simply followed us on our @patternity Instagram — we are infinitely grateful to our global community of collaborators, founding members, friends, family, and inspirers who have believed in and supported our journey so far.

"Let us be grateful to the people who make us happy; they are the charming gardeners who make our souls blossom."

Marcel Proust (1871–1922), French novelist

# A few people who have been a special part
## of our own grateful journeys

Judith, Andy, Tor, Dave, Kate, Robin, Nick, Jonathan, Sophie, Grace, Willow, Joan, Mabel, and the marvellous Murray Clan.

Vicki, Toby, George, Moss, Kate, Claire, Jess, and all the wonderful Winteringhams.

Aaro Murphy, Alex Tieghi-Walker, Alice Gee, Alice Kavanagh, Andres Roberts, Anna Day, Bec Rainford, Bonny Tydeman, Carmen De-Baets, Catherine Björksten, Charlotte McConnell, Charlotte Pawson, Chris Connors, Chris Pawson, Christopher Nield, Colin Henderson, Daisy Ellison, Dal Chodha, David Davies, Dawn Griffiths, Debs, Derek Pawson, Elizabeth Ferguson, Emily Stone, Emma Sutton, Emmie Sharp, Flora Parkinson, FNAF, Fran Myatt, Fritjof Capra, Grace Gallagher, Halla Kousi, Helena Hobbs, Holly Ferguson, Ian Quest, India Burr-Hersey, James Mason, Jeff Gilbert, Jemma Ruddock, Jeremy Lent, Jess Meyer, Jessie Brinton, Jill Gate, Jnanavaca, Jodi Pawson, Joe Wood, Johanna Pemberton, John Ashworth, John P. Milton, Jude Stewart, Julio Cesar, Kajedo Wanderer, Kate Todd, Kathryn Younger, Land Of Plenty, Leslie Pawson, Lily and Ray, Lisa O'Reilly, Lisa Piercy, Louisa Ziane, Lucy Hill, Lucy Murray, Lulu Roper-Caldbeck, Mandy Adams, Maria Kennedy, Marojlein Govaerts, Martijn Sjoorda, Martyn Moutinho, Nadine Alford, Neil Pemberton, Nick Curnow, Obonjan, Paul Burton, Paul Cullington, Paul Isaac, Philippa Prinsloo, Rebecca Petts Davies, Rhona Clews, Rhonda Drakeford, Rosie Lom, Sabine Zetteler, Sally Forster, Sally Holt, Sarah Ruddock, Sophie Portas, Stefano Colombini, Susan Rozo, Susi Paz, Sylvy Early, Tas Elias, Thalia Pawson, Tim Anscombe-Bell, Tim Williams, Tom Russell, Tony Glazzard, Tula Anastasiades, Vickie Hayward, Vidyadaka, Wynne Griffiths, and You're Gorgeous!

An extra special thanks to our commissioning editor Elen Jones at Ebury Publishing; Penguin Random House for approaching us with the concept of this journal; Dr. Elle Parker for your insights and advice with the content; Jamie and Judith for your endless grateful inspiration and support; Claire and Gavin, our instrumental agents at ITB; Will and Jenny at Atwork for your design expertise; Gemma Jones and Steph Wood for your essential encouragement; and last but by no means least our head of research Liv Taylor for being such an integral part of the weird and wonderful journey that is PATTERNITY.

A final thank-you to all the magnificent makers who have been involved in the creation of this journal — from the trees to the printers, copyeditors, and binders — we are so grateful.

# Grateful Resources

We wanted to share a few of the resources that have inspired and shaped our own grateful journey so far:

## TO WATCH

- *Want to be happy? Be grateful* – David Steindl-Rast: TED.com
- *Powers of Ten™* (1977) – YouTube
- *How Wolves Change Rivers* – YouTube
- *You're It* – Alan Watts – YouTube
- *Samsara* – Ron Fricke and Mark Magidson
- *365 Grateful project* – Hailey Bartholomew
- *The Overview Effect* – Planetary collective
- *Nature, Beauty, Gratitude* – Louie Schwartzberg:TED.com
- *An Ecology of Mind* – Gregory Bateson
- *The Wisdom Keepers* – Paqo Andino (Jeffry Wium)

## TO READ

- Beck, Charlotte – *Everyday Zen*
- Capra, Fritjof – *Web of Life*
- Carson, Rachel – *The Sense of Wonder*
- De Botton, Alain – *Religion for Atheists*
- Fromm, Eric – *The Art of Being*
- Gooley, Tristan – *How to Connect with Nature*
- Haidt, Jonathan – *The Happiness Hypothesis*
- Haekel, Ernst – *Art Forms in Nature*
- Harari, Yuval Noah – *Sapiens*
- Hosey, Lance – *The Shape of Green*

- HRH the Prince of Wales – *Harmony*
- Jowarski, Joseph – *Synchronicity*
- Koren, Leonard – *Wabi Sabi*
- Lent, Jeremy – *The Patterning Instinct*
- Milton, John P. – *Sky Above Earth Below*
- Moore, Alan – *Do Design*
- O'Hara, Gwydion – *Pagan Ways*
- Reddy, Jini – *Wild Times*
- Stew, Jude – *Patternalia*
- Sacks, Oliver – *Gratitude*
- Vitti, Alisa – *Woman Code*
- Watts, Alan – *Nature, Man and Woman*
- Wimala, Bhante Y. – *Lessons of the Lotus*
- Wohlleben, Peter – *The Hidden Life of Trees*

## TO EXPLORE — BOTH ONLINE AND OFFLINE

- FritjofCapra.net
- WayofNature.co.uk
- Innerspace.org.uk
- TheSchoolofLife.com
- findhorn.org
- alternatives.org.uk
- actionforhappiness.org
- PATTERNITY.org
- obonjan-island.com
- schumachercollege.org.uk

"What we call a part is merely a pattern in an inseparable web of relationships."

Fritjof Capra (b. 1939), physicist and ecologist

# PATTERNITY

## Inspiring positive living through pattern research, design, and experience

Since launching in 2009, PATTERNITY has received international recognition for its research-based approach to pattern design and experience. PATTERNITY has collaborated with a range of multidisciplinary partners and specialists across the globe — from science to spirituality, wellbeing to the arts — to explore the visual and non-visual patterns that shape personal experience and culture at large. In addition to its pattern-focused products and projects, PATTERNITY hosts regular research-based events for its loyal community of design and pattern enthusiasts seeking to find purpose and positivity and re-engage with their inner creativity.

To find out more visit patternity.org
or connect via social media:
Twitter @patternitweet
Instagram and Facebook @patternity

"Because a shared awareness
and understanding of pattern
will positively shape the future."

PATTERNITY

# Introducing Your Free-Flow Pages

## Write, Draw, Create

Please feel free to use these pages for whatever
you wish — scribble, jot, explore …

"Everything flows, nothing stands still."

Heraclitus of Ephesus (c. 535–475 BC), Greek philosopher

"Wonder is the beginning of wisdom."

Greek Proverb

Andrews McMeel Publishing
a division of Andrews McMeel Universal
1130 Walnut Street, Kansas City, Missouri 64106

www.andrewsmcmeel.com

18 19 20 21 22 SDB 10 9 8 7 6 5 4 3 2 1

ISBN: 978-1-4494-9185-7

*Be Great Be Grateful* was first published in
Great Britain in 2017 by Ebury Press, a
division of Penguin Random House UK.

Library of Congress Control Number: 2017951695

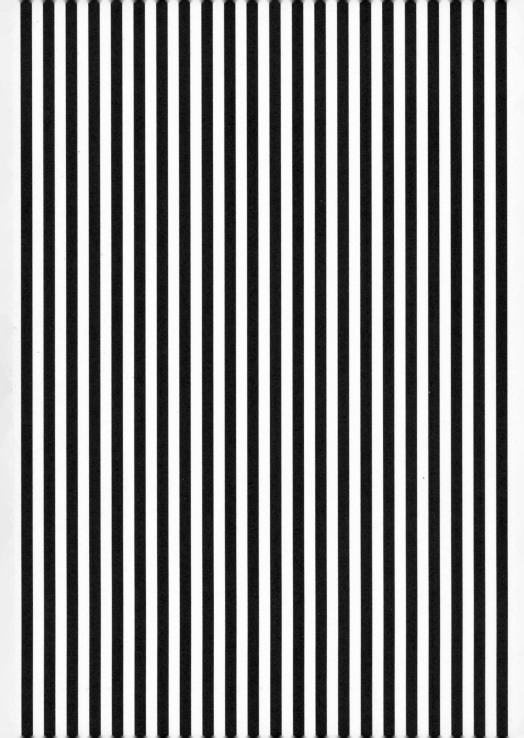